I WONDER WHY

The Sun Rises

KINGFISHER
LONDON & NEW YORK

Copyright © Macmillan Publishers
International Ltd 2011, 2023
Published in the United States by Kingfisher
120 Broadway, New York, NY 10271
Kingfisher is a division of Macmillan
Children's Books, London

ISBN: 978-0-7534-7922-3 (HB)
ISBN: 978-0-7534-7921-6 (PB)

Distributed in the U.S. and Canada by Macmillan,
120 Broadway, New York, NY 10271

EU representative: Macmillan Publishers Ireland Ltd,
1st Floor, The Liffey Trust Centre, 117-126 Sheriff
Street Upper, Dublin 1, D01 YC43.

Library of Congress Cataloging-in-Publication
data has been applied for.

Author: Brenda Walpole
Consultant: Ian Graham

2023 edition
Editor: Seeta Parmar
Designer: Peter Clayman
Design Assistant: Amelia Brooks
Illustrator: Marie-Eve Tremblay

Kingfisher books are available for special
promotions and premiums. For details contact:
Special Markets Department, Macmillan,
120 Broadway, New York, NY 10271.

For more information, please visit
www.kingfisherbooks.com.

Printed in China
9 8 7 6 5 4 3 2
2TR/0723/WKT/RV/128MA

CONTENTS

Why does the Sun rise in the morning?

The Sun doesn't actually rise at all! It's Earth that turns around to give us **a sunrise each morning**. Earth is like a **spinning** ball. Wherever you are, it starts to get light as your part of Earth spins around to face the Sun. The **sky grows brighter** and it is morning.

Every morning, the Sun rises in the east. Its light wakes animals early. A new day begins.

The weather may be gray and gloomy, but above the clouds, the Sun is always shining.

Why does it get dark at night?

Earth keeps spinning all day long. As it moves, the Sun seems to **travel across the sky**. As the hours pass, your part of Earth turns farther away from the Sun. The Sun seems to sink in the sky and darkness comes. It is night.

It takes 24 hours for Earth to turn around once. While one half has daylight, the other half has night.

At night, one side of Earth is in deep shadow. This makes it feel much cooler, so you often need to wrap up warm.

Where is it night all day long?

During the **winter** months, the lands around the poles don't see the Sun at all. The Sun is so low in the sky that it's hidden below the horizon. This makes the days **cold and dark**—even at noon.

Winter days are dark in the northern lands of Scandinavia. Sami, or Lapp, children go to school by the light of the Moon and stars.

Some people are so miserable in the dark days of winter that they get sick. Doctors call this seasonal affective disorder (SAD) and find that special types of bright lights often make their patients feel better.

During the summer, it is very different at the poles. The Sun is in the sky morning, noon, and night. For the seals, it must be like sleeping with the lights on.

After the dark days of winter, it must be wonderful to see the Sun again. The Inuit people of North America used to celebrate its return by lighting new lamps in their homes.

Where do all the days start on time?

In tropical lands near the **equator**, the Sun rises at almost the same time every morning. And it sets at almost the same time every evening! The days and nights are each about **12 hours long**—every single day of the year.

Why do we have seasons?

We have seasons because of the way Earth **spins** around, or orbits, the Sun. Each orbit takes one year from start to finish. Earth is **tilted**, and as the planet orbits, first one pole and then the other leans toward the Sun. This is what gives us the **seasons**.

In September, neither pole leans toward the Sun. There is fall in the north and spring in the south.

In December, the North Pole leans away from the Sun. The northern half of Earth has winter. The southern half has summer.

EQUATOR

The weather is always hot at the equator because the Sun is high overhead. But at the poles, the Sun is lower in the sky. Its rays are spread out and feel much weaker.

The seasons are different in the northern and southern halves of Earth. Depending on where you are, wearing a swimsuit in December could give you frostbite or a sunburn!

In June, the North Pole leans toward the Sun. The northern half of Earth has summer. The southern half has winter.

In March, neither pole leans toward the Sun. There is spring in the north and fall in the south.

NORTH POLE

Earth spins around as it orbits the Sun. It doesn't spin upright, however, but tilts to one side.

SOUTH POLE

Why do we plant seeds in spring?

Seeds need to be warm and wet before they can sprout. As the spring sunshine starts to **warm the ground**, farmers and gardeners dig the soil and sow their **seeds**. The plants don't take long to grow.

Why are bees busy in summer?

On **warm, sunny days,** bees are busy visiting hundreds of flowers. Inside each flower is a drop of **sugar-sweet nectar.** Bees feed on it and use it to make honey back at their hive.

Bees can see patterns and colors on flower petals that we can't see. They guide the bees in like landing lights on an airport runway.

Why do leaves drop in the fall?

Not all trees lose their leaves. Conifers have tough leaves that can stand the winter cold.

In fall, trees find it difficult to suck up water from the **cold, frozen ground,** so their leaves dry out. The leaves turn red, gold and brown and fall to the ground, leaving the trees bare for winter. The trees will grow **new leaves** in the spring.

Why do animals sleep through the winter?

For some animals, sleeping is the best way to **survive** the hungry winter days. Chipmunks, hedgehogs, and some bears eat as much as they can in the fall and then sleep **somewhere safe** until the spring.

Many animals grow thick winter coats to help them survive the bitter cold, such as the moose.

Where are there only two seasons?

Many tropical countries have only two seasons every year. One is very **wet**, and the other is very **dry**. Not many trees manage to survive the dry months, and animals travel hundreds of miles **searching** for food and water.

In the dry season, herds of wildebeests and zebras cross the grasslands of central Africa. They follow the thunderclouds in search of rainwater and fresh grass.

During the dry season, the ground is baked hard by the hot sun. Clouds of dust cover everything and everyone.

Many animals migrate in different seasons. Every year, swarms of monarch butterflies leave Mexico and fly 3,000 miles (4,800km) to spend the summer by cool Canadian lakes.

Where does it pour for a month?

Some parts of India and Southeast Asia have long, heavy downpours called **monsoons**. Big black clouds are blown in from the sea during the summer months. Once the rain starts, it can last for weeks, **flooding** fields and streets.

Who can tell the time without a clock?

We all can! Inside every one of us there's something called a **body clock**. It wakes us up every morning and tells us that it's breakfast time. And throughout the day, we seem to know when it's time to work, eat, and play. As evening comes, we feel tired and get ready to sleep.

Newborn babies don't know their days from their nights. They just wake up their parents whenever they feel hungry!

Different kinds of animals live to different kinds of clocks. A bee and a badger never meet. One is active by day, while the other is active at night.

Can flowers tell the time?

A few flowers are such good **timekeepers** that they open at the same time every day. Gardeners sometimes plant flowers like these in **flower clocks**. There are as many as 12 different flowers in one "clock," and they open one after the other as the hours pass.

Can animals tell the time?

Some wild animals are active by day, and others wake up only at night. They can't tell the time of **day or night**, but some animals do know the time of year. Animals have body clocks, too. In zoos and on farms, many of them know when it's feeding time.

The Canadian snowshoe hare knows when winter's coming. It grows a white fur coat to hide from foxes when the snow arrives.

Which calendar was carved in stone?

Many hundreds of years ago, people called the **Aztecs** lived in **Central America**. They made a calendar from a huge stone shaped like the Sun. The face of the Sun god was **carved** in the middle, and signs for the days were carved all around the edge.

The Aztec calendar stone measured almost 13 feet (4m) from side to side—that's far too big to hang on a wall!

Who invented our calendar?

More than 2,000 years ago, a Roman ruler named **Julius Caesar** invented the calendar that we use today. He gave each year **365 days** and arranged them in 12 months. Since then, the calendar has hardly changed.

What is a leap year?

Every four years we have what we call a leap year. This is a year with 366 days instead of 365. The **extra day** is added at the end of February. So if your birthday falls on **February 29th**, it's a very special day indeed.

A leap year can always be divided by four, with none left over. The years 2024, 2028, and 2032 are all leap years.

Why do we need calendars?

Most of us need calendars to help us **remember** all the things we plan in a year. But they also help us keep track of time. When people are stuck without a clock they find different ways to mark the passing days.

Who Lights The Lamps At New Year?

Diwali is one of many Hindu New Year festivals. It is also called the **Festival of Light**—and no wonder! Towns are strung with lights, and lamps shine from every door and window. People make **beautiful** floor pictures with colored chalks, flour, and sand, and decorate them with glowing candles.

Some Hindu New Year festivals occur in the fall, while others are celebrated in early spring.

Who blows a horn at New Year?

Rosh Hashanah falls in October or November. People eat apples and bread dipped in honey in the hope of a sweet year to come!

The Jewish New Year festival of Rosh Hashanah begins with the blowing of a curly **ram's horn**. The sound calls people to the synagogue to pray for God's **forgiveness** for the things they've done wrong in the past year. As the new year begins they can make a fresh start.

Who brings in the New Year with a bang?

The new year in China starts with beating drums, **crashing cymbals**, fireworks, and a lion or dragon dancing through the streets. All this noise is supposed to chase away the bad days of the past and bring luck in the future.

Chinese new year celebrations can last up to 15 days. They begin between the middle of January and the middle of February.

How long is a month?

On today's **calendars**, a month can be as short as 28 days or as long as 31 days. But in the past, a month was the time between one **full moon** and the next. Every month was exactly the same length, and that was 29.5 days.

The first man on the Moon was Neil Armstrong, an American astronaut who took part in the Apollo 11 space mission in July 1969.

The Moon is a dark, lifeless world. It looks bright because one side is always lit up by the Sun. What we call moonlight is really reflected sunlight.

In East Asian folklore there is a rabbit on the Moon.

Why does the Moon change shape?

The Moon doesn't really change shape. What changes is the shape of the **sunlit** part of the Moon that you can see from Earth. As the Moon moves around Earth in its **orbit**, the Sun lights it from different directions. First the bright side seems to **grow**, and then it seems to shrink.

Who eats the Moon?

Children in China eat **delicious** moon-shaped cakes for the Moon-viewing festival. At the September full moon, families walk to the park carrying lanterns. Then they eat their cakes and **admire** the Moon!

One piece of music by the German composer Beethoven was nicknamed the "Moonlight Sonata." You can imagine the Moon rising as you listen to it.

Why are there seven days in a week?

No one's quite sure how there came to be seven days in a week. Long ago, it may have been the **time** between one market day and another, or maybe it was just a quarter of a moon month. But after all this time, a seven-day week feels just about **right**.

When is it 13 o'clock?

After 12 o'clock, of course! Clocks that **number** the hours from 1 to 24 are known as **24-hour clocks**. Until midday, the hours are numbered 1 to 12. After midday, we just carry on **counting**.

The ancient Greeks had a ten-day week. It was a long wait until the weekend!

The first clocks and sundials showed only the hours. Nowadays people need to know the time to the nearest minute —to catch trains on time, for example!

A minute isn't long—it's just enough time to peel an apple! There are 60 seconds in a minute and 60 minutes in an hour. The number 60 was chosen more than **5,000 years ago**, probably because so many different numbers go into it evenly.

We split the week into workdays and rest days. After five hard days at school, everyone loves the weekend!

Why does my watch tick?

More than 20 tiny wheels are packed neatly inside a watch. You can hear them **tick and tock** as the teeth of one wheel lock into the teeth of the next. The moving **wheels** keep time and slowly turn the hands around the watch face.

How did people manage before clocks?

Before clocks were invented, people told the **time** by looking at the **Sun**. They got up at sunrise and went to bed when it was dark. They ate lunch when the Sun was high up above and ate dinner when it set in the west.

How does a grandfather keep good time?

A tall grandfather clock has a long pendulum that swings back and forth in a steady **rhythm**. With every swing, wheels inside the clock slowly turn, moving the **hands** around the face. Winding the clock with a key stops it from slowing down.

Sundials are one of the oldest kinds of clocks. Instead of a moving hand, they have a shadow cast by the Sun. As Earth turns during the day, the "hand" moves around the clock.

How can you split a second?

Today's electronic timers are so accurate that they can split a second into a **million** parts. In competitions, athletes are timed to a hundredth of a second—that's less than the time it takes for you to **blink**.

Which timer was a load of old rope?

About 400 years ago, a ship's **speed** was measured with a log tied to a knotted rope. The sailors threw the log overboard and counted how many **knots** unwound as the ship moved forward. They used an hourglass to accurately time it. Today, **sailors** still measure a ship's speed in knots. One knot is just under 1.3 miles per hour (2km/h).

How can you cook an egg with sand?

Four minutes is all it takes for the sand inside an **egg-timer** to run from the top to the bottom. And that's just the right time to soft-boil an egg. Hourglasses are **simple and accurate** and have been used for hundreds of years. Once the timer has finished, you just turn it upside down to start again!

What's the time on Earth?

What time it is depends on where you are! At exactly the same moment, **clocks** around the world tell completely **different times**. Every country sets its own time so that it's noon when the Sun is highest in the sky. That way, everyone gets up when it's getting light and goes to sleep when it's dark.

Alaska, USA
It's seven o'clock. It's the start of a new day.

Alaska

New York

New York, USA
It's noon—time to think about lunch!

Traveling across time zones can confuse your body clock. Air passengers may have breakfast in London, England, fly to New York, and arrive in time for . . . a second breakfast!

Central Siberia, Russia
It's midnight. The day is over.

To keep track of time, Earth has been split up into 24 slices, like stripes on a beach ball. These are time zones, and there is one zone for each hour of the day. Some big countries have more than one time zone.

3

2

Siberia

1

12

11

What's the time in space?

10

It must be difficult to tell time when you're in space—a **clock won't work**, and you can't use the Moon, Earth, or the Sun! Astronauts **stay in touch** with base and follow a particular Earth time. It's their radio, not their clock, that tells them the time!

9

8

Lagos

7

6

5

4

Lagos, Nigeria
It's 6 o'clock. All the children are home from school.

How long does a person live?

Most of us will **enjoy many birthdays** as long as we stay fit and healthy. Humans live about the same length of time as elephants, ravens, and some parrots!

How long does a mayfly live?

A mayfly lives only for **about a day**. It unfolds its wings for the first time in the morning and folds them for the last time at night. That's just long enough for mayflies to mate and lay their eggs before they die.

Mayflies have been around for more than 300 million years. That's older than the dinosaurs!

Most women live longer than men. The oldest person ever was a woman who lived to be over 120 years old.

How long does a tree live?

Trees grow **very slowly** and have long lives. Most trees live for between 100 and 250 years, but some bristlecone pines are more than **4,500 years old**. They are some of the oldest living things on Earth.

Trees make new wood every year and leave a telltale ring in their trunk. Counting the rings on a tree stump tells you how old the tree was when it was cut down.

INDEX